VOL. 3

HAL•LEONARD®

TRUMPET PLAY-ALONG

AUDIO ACCESS INCLUDED

# Classic Rock

CW01584366

To access audio visit:
**www.halleonard.com/mylibrary**

Enter Code
2774-2104-5176-2319

ISBN 978-1-4950-0013-3

For all works contained herein:
Unauthorized copying, arranging, adapting, recording, Internet posting, public performance, or other distribution of the printed or recorded music in this publication is an infringement of copyright.
Infringers are liable under the law.

Visit Hal Leonard Online at
**www.halleonard.com**

HAL•LEONARD®
CORPORATION
7777 W. BLUEMOUND RD. P.O. BOX 13819
MILWAUKEE, WISCONSIN 53213

# Classic Rock

CONTENTS


4 All You Need Is Love
THE BEATLES

8 Deacon Blues
STEELY DAN

12 Feelin' Stronger Every Day
CHICAGO

18 Higher Love
STEVE WINDWOOD

28 September
EARTH, WIND & FIRE

34 Spinning Wheel
BLOOD, SWEAT & TEARS

25 25 or 6 to 4
CHICAGO

40 Vehicle
IDES OF MARCH

# All You Need Is Love

Words and Music by John Lennon and Paul McCartney

Copyright © 1967 Sony/ATV Music Publishing LLC
Copyright Renewed
All Rights Administered by Sony/ATV Music Publishing LLC, 424 Church Street, Suite 1200, Nashville, TN 37219
International Copyright Secured All Rights Reserved

E E/D 1. C♯m7 E 2. C♯m7 E
eas - y.
A B7 E A B7
All you need is love.
All you need is love.
mp
E A C♯7 F♯m Amaj7/E
All you need is love, love.
Dmaj7 E A N.C. A E/G♯ F♯m7 N.C.
Love is all you need.
Guitar:
f
A E/G♯ F♯m7 N.C. E7/B A
Strings:
mp
G♯dim G♯dim/F♯ E E/D C♯m7 E
A B7 E A B7
All you need is love.
All you need is love.
Trumpet:
f

E A C#7 F#m Amaj7/E
All you need is love, love.
Dmaj7 E A N.C. A E/G#
Love is all you need. Noth-ing you can know that is-n't
F#m7 N.C. A E/G# F#m7 N.C.
known; noth-ing you can see that is-n't shown;
E7/B A E7/G# E7/F#
no-where you can be that is-n't where you're meant to be; it's
E E/D C#m7 E A B7 E
eas-y. All you need is love.
A B7 E A C#7
All you need is love. All you need is love,
2nd time 8va
F#m Amaj7/E 1. Dmaj7 E A N.C.
love. Love is all you need.

2.
Dmaj7
E
A
Love is all you need. Love is all you need. Love is all
(Love is all you need.
you need. Love is all you need. Love is all
Love is all you need. Love is all you need.
you need. Love is all you need. Love is all
Love is all you need. Love is all you need.
Trumpet:
staccato
f
you need. Love is all you need. Love is all
Love is all you need. Love is all you need.
you need. Love is all you need. Love is all
Love is all you need. Love is all you need.
Repeat ad lib. and Fade
you need. Love is all you need. Love is all
Love is all you need. Love is all you need.

# Deacon Blues

Words and Music by Walter Becker and Donald Fagen

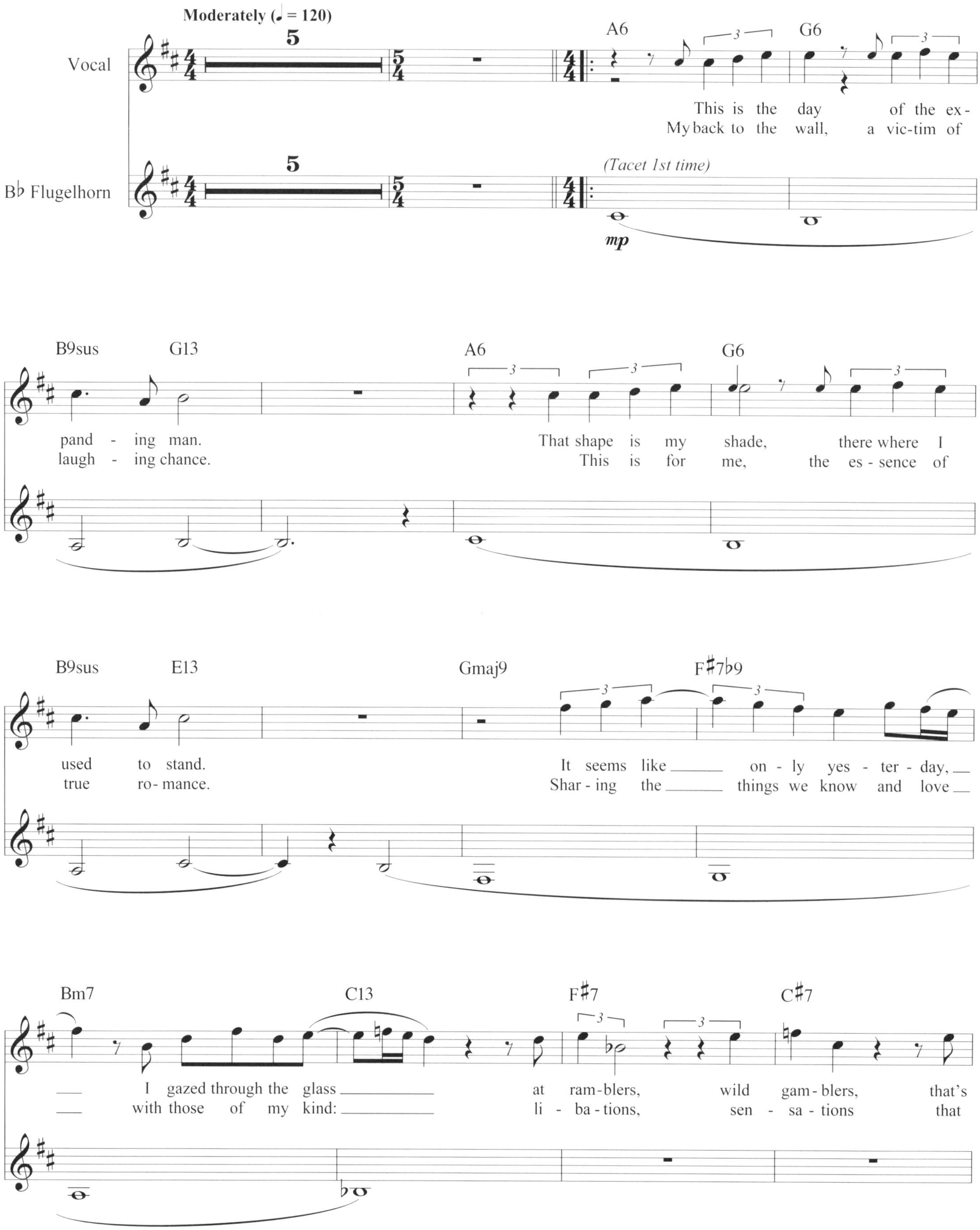


Copyright © 1977, 1978 UNIVERSAL MUSIC CORP.
Copyright Renewed
All Rights Reserved Used by Permission

C♯m7♭5 F♯7 C♯ F♯7♯9 A G
all in the past. You call me a fool, you say it's a
stag - ger the mind. I crawl like a vip - er through these sub -
This is the night of the ex -
B13sus G13 A G
cra - zy scheme. This one's for real, I al - read - y
ur - ban streets, make love to these wom - en, lan - guid and
pand - ing man. I take one last drag as I ap -
(Tacet 1st time)
B9sus B13 Gmaj9 F♯7♯9
bought the dream. So use - less to ask me why.
bit - ter - sweet. I'll rise when the sun goes down,
proach the stand. I cried when I wrote this song,
Bm7 Am9 A♭9♯5 Gmaj13
Throw a kiss and say good - bye. I'll make it this
cov - er ev - 'ry game in town. A world of my
sue me if I play too long. This broth - er is
D(add9)/F♯ E13 A13sus A9
time. I'm read - y to cross that fine line.
own, I'll make it my home sweet home.
free. I'll be what I want to be.

Bm7 F♯m7 Em7 Dmaj9
Learn to work the sax - o - phone, I play just what I feel.
Cmaj9 Bm7 A6 A♭7♭5 Gmaj9 Dsus2/F♯ D/G
Drink scotch whis-key all night long and die be - hind the wheel.
Bm7 F♯m7 Em7
They got a name for the win - ners in the world, I want a name
Dmaj9 Cmaj9 Bm7 A(add9)
when I lose. They call Al - a - bam - a the Crim - son Tide,
A♭7♭5 Gmaj7 Dsus2/F♯ Gmaj7 Bm7 F♯m7
call me Dea - con Blues.
mf
p

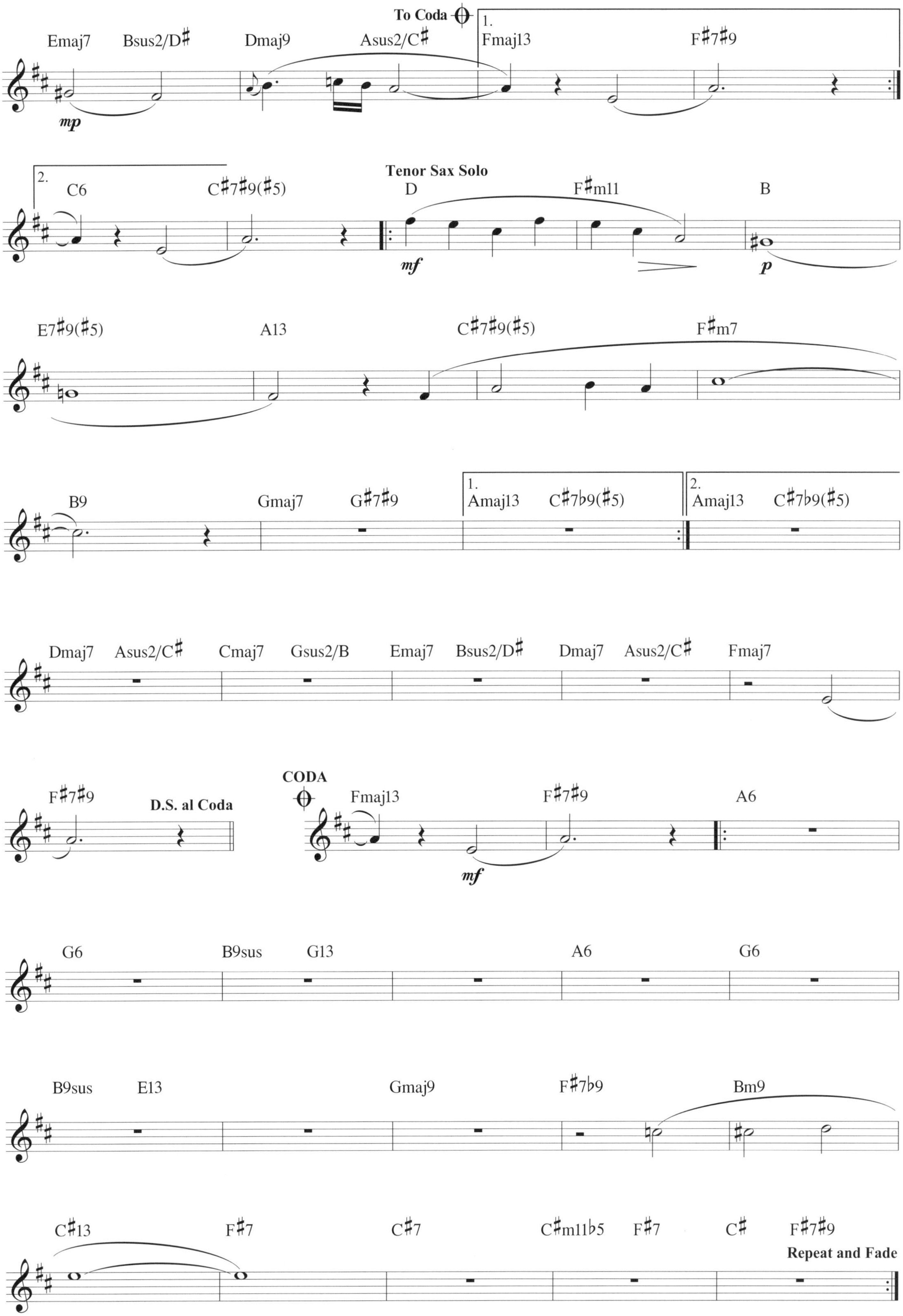
To Coda
1.
Emaj7 Bsus2/D♯ Dmaj9 Asus2/C♯ Fmaj13 F♯7♯9
mp
2.
C6 C♯7♯9(♯5)
Tenor Sax Solo
D F♯m11 B
mf
p
E7♯9(♯5) A13 C♯7♯9(♯5) F♯m7
B9 Gmaj7 G♯7♯9
1.
Amaj13 C♯7♭9(♯5)
2.
Amaj13 C♯7♭9(♯5)
Dmaj7 Asus2/C♯ Cmaj7 Gsus2/B Emaj7 Bsus2/D♯ Dmaj7 Asus2/C♯ Fmaj7
F♯7♯9
D.S. al Coda
CODA
Fmaj13 F♯7♯9 A6
mf
G6 B9sus G13 A6 G6
B9sus E13 Gmaj9 F♯7♭9 Bm9
C♯13 F♯7 C♯7 C♯m11♭5 F♯7 C♯ F♯7♯9
Repeat and Fade

# Feelin' Stronger Every Day

Words and Music by Peter Cetera and James Pankow

Copyright © 1973 by Universal Music - MGB Songs, Primary Wave Pankow and Big Elk Music
Copyright Renewed
All Rights for Primary Wave Pankow Administered by BMG Rights Management (US) LLC
International Copyright Secured All Rights Reserved

F/C C/E G D
Oh, yeah. And now we've
F C
re - al - ized love's not all that it's s'posed to be.
F/C C/E G F/C C/E G
Oh, yeah. Oh, yeah.
Bm7 Em7
And know - ing that you would have want - ed it this way,
Bm7 Em7 G A
I do be - lieve I'm feel - in' strong - er ev - 'ry day.

D
I know we real - ly tried, to -
F
C
F/C C/E G
geth - er we had a love in - side. Oh, yeah.
F/C C/E G
D
Oh, yeah. So now the time
F
C
has come for both of us to live on the run.
F/C C/E G
F/C C/E G
Oh, yeah. Oh, yeah.

Bm7
Em7
And know - ing that you would have want - ed it this way,
Bm7
Em7 G A
I do be - lieve I'm feel - in' stron - ger ev - 'ry day.
D G
Yeah, yeah, yeah.
Em7 G A
D G
Yeah, yeah, yeah.
D
yeah.
Huh.

Bright Rock (same tempo) (♩ = 152)
B F♯ C♯ G♯ D♯ C♯ B F♯ C♯ G♯ D♯ C♯
Trumpet:
Af - ter what you meant to me,
ooh, ba - by now,
I can make it eas - i - ly.
I know that we both agree,
the best thing to hap - pen to you,
the best thing that hap - pen'd to me.
Yeah, yeah,

B
F♯
C♯
yeah.
(Vocal tacet 2nd time)
Feel - in' stron - ger ev - 'ry day.
Play 10 Times and Fade

# Higher Love

Words and Music by Will Jennings and Steve Winwood

Copyright © 1986 BLUE SKY RIDER SONGS, F.S. MUSIC LTD. and KOBALT MUSIC COPYRIGHTS SARL
All Rights for BLUE SKY RIDER SONGS Administered by IRVING MUSIC, INC.
All Rights Reserved Used by Permission

D C G
We walk blind, though we try to see.
D Bm Em To Coda
Fall - ing be - hind in what could be.
C G D Em C G
Bring me a high - er love. Bring me a high - er love,
D Em C G D Em
whoa. Bring me a high - er love. Where's that
C G Em D
high - er love I keep think - in' of? Worlds are turn -

C G F G
-in', and we're just hang-in' on. Fac-
F C Am G
-ing our fear and stand-in' out there a-lone. A yearn-
C G F G
-in', and it's real to me. There
(Synth. cues)
p
F C G D Em
must be some-one who's feel-in' for me.
mf
D.S. al Coda

CODA
C G D Em C G
Bring me a high - er love. Bring me a high - er love,
D Em C G D Em
whoa. Bring me a high - er love.
Where's that
I could
1. C G Em D
high - er love I keep think - in' of?
2. C G
rise a - bove on a
Em D C/D D Em D C C/D Em(add4)
high - er love. I will wait for it. I'm not
Em D C C/D Em D C
too late for it. Un - til then, I'll sing my song

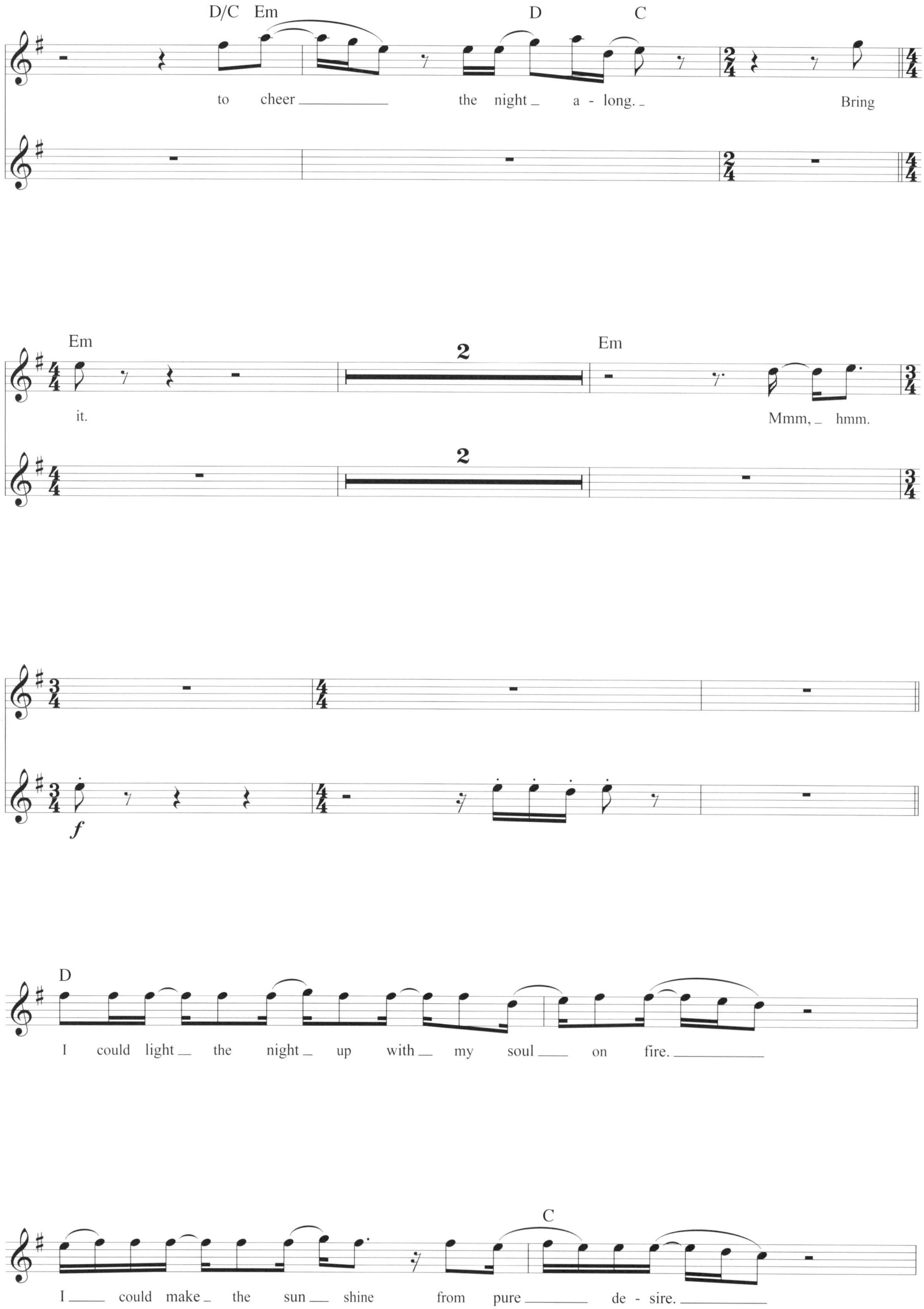
D/C Em D C
to cheer the night a - long. Bring
Em 2 Em
it. Mmm, hmm.
D
I could light the night up with my soul on fire.
C
I could make the sun shine from pure de - sire.

Em F C
Let me feel that love come o - ver me.
mp
Em C G D
Let me feel how strong it should be.
3
3
N.C. C G D Em
Whoa, bring me a high - er love.
C G D Em C G
Bring me a high - er love, whoa. Bring me a high - er love.
D Em C G Em D
Where's that high - er love I keep think - in' of?

4
N.C.
(Bring me a high - er love.
Bring me a high - er love,
oh.)
Bring it, babe. (Bring me a high - er love.)
C
G
D
Em
Oh...
(Bring me a high - er love.)
Play 3 times and Fade
(Bring me a high - er love.
(Lead vocal ad lib.)
Bring me a high - er love,
oh.
Fadeout (3rd time)
Bring me a high - er love.
Bring me a high - er love.)
1.
2.

# 25 or 6 to 4

Words and Music by Robert Lamm

Copyright (c) 1970 Lamminations Music, Aurelius Music and Spirit Catalog Holdings, S.a.r.l.
Copyright Renewed
All Rights for Lamminations Music Administered by BMG Rights Management (US) LLC
All Rights for Aurelius Music Controlled and Administered throughout the world by Spirit Two Music, Inc.
All Rights for Spirit Catalog Holdings, S.a.r.l. Controlled and Administered in the U.S., Canada, UK and Eire by Spirit Two Music, Inc.
All Rights for Spirit Catalog Holdings, S.a.r.l. Controlled and Administered throughout the world excluding the U.S., Canada, UK and Eire by Spirit Services Holdings S.a.r.l.
International Copyright Secured All Rights Reserved

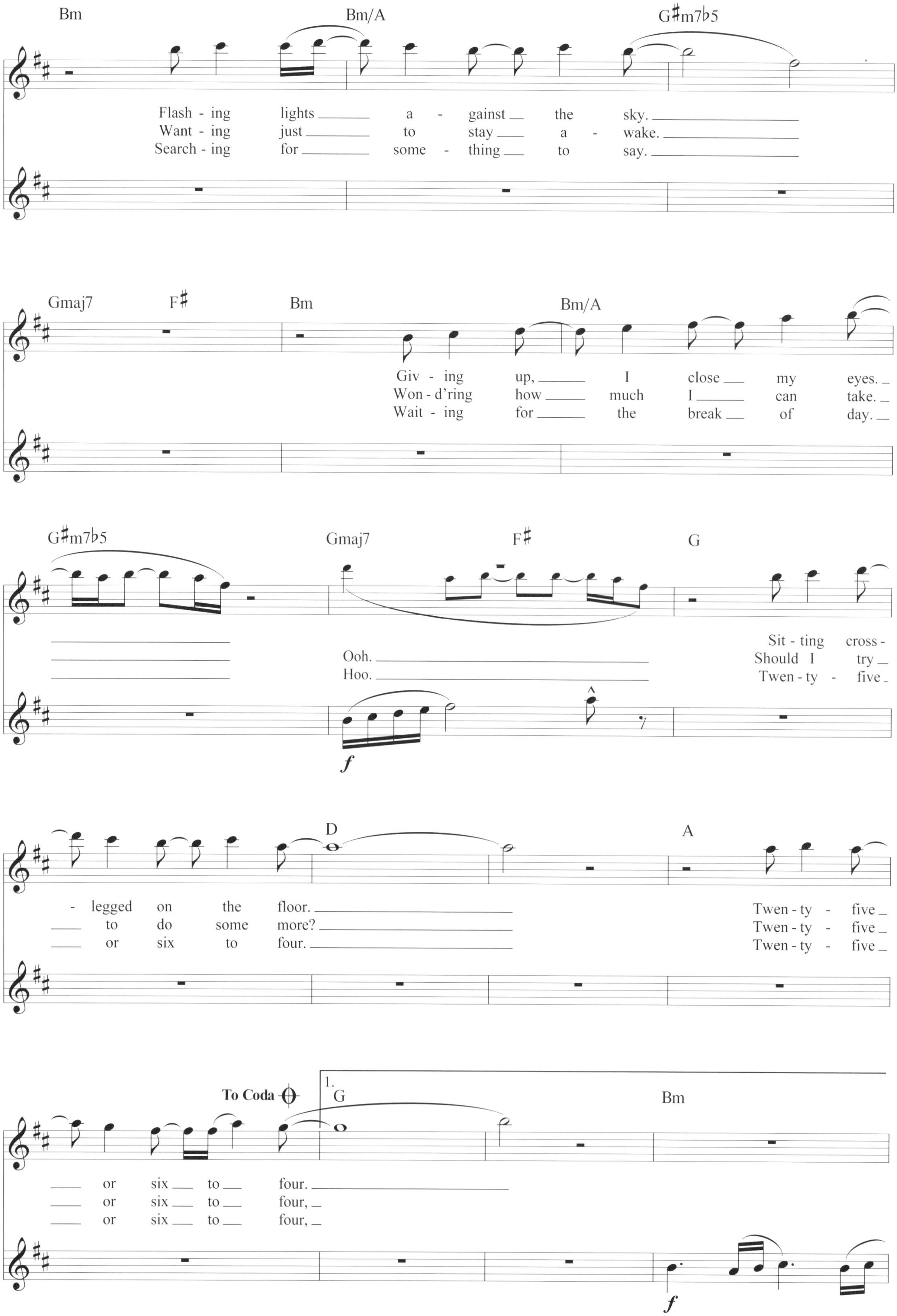
Bm
Bm/A
G♯m7♭5
Flash - ing lights a - gainst the sky.
Want - ing just to stay a - wake.
Search - ing for some - thing to say.
Gmaj7
F♯
Bm
Bm/A
Giv - ing up, I close my eyes.
Won - d'ring how much I can take.
Wait - ing for the break of day.
G♯m7♭5
Gmaj7
F♯
G
Ooh.
Hoo.
Sit - ting cross - legged on the floor.
Should I try to do some more?
Twen - ty - five or six to four.
D
A
Twen - ty - five or six to four.
Twen - ty - five or six to four,
Twen - ty - five or six to four,
To Coda
1.
G
Bm

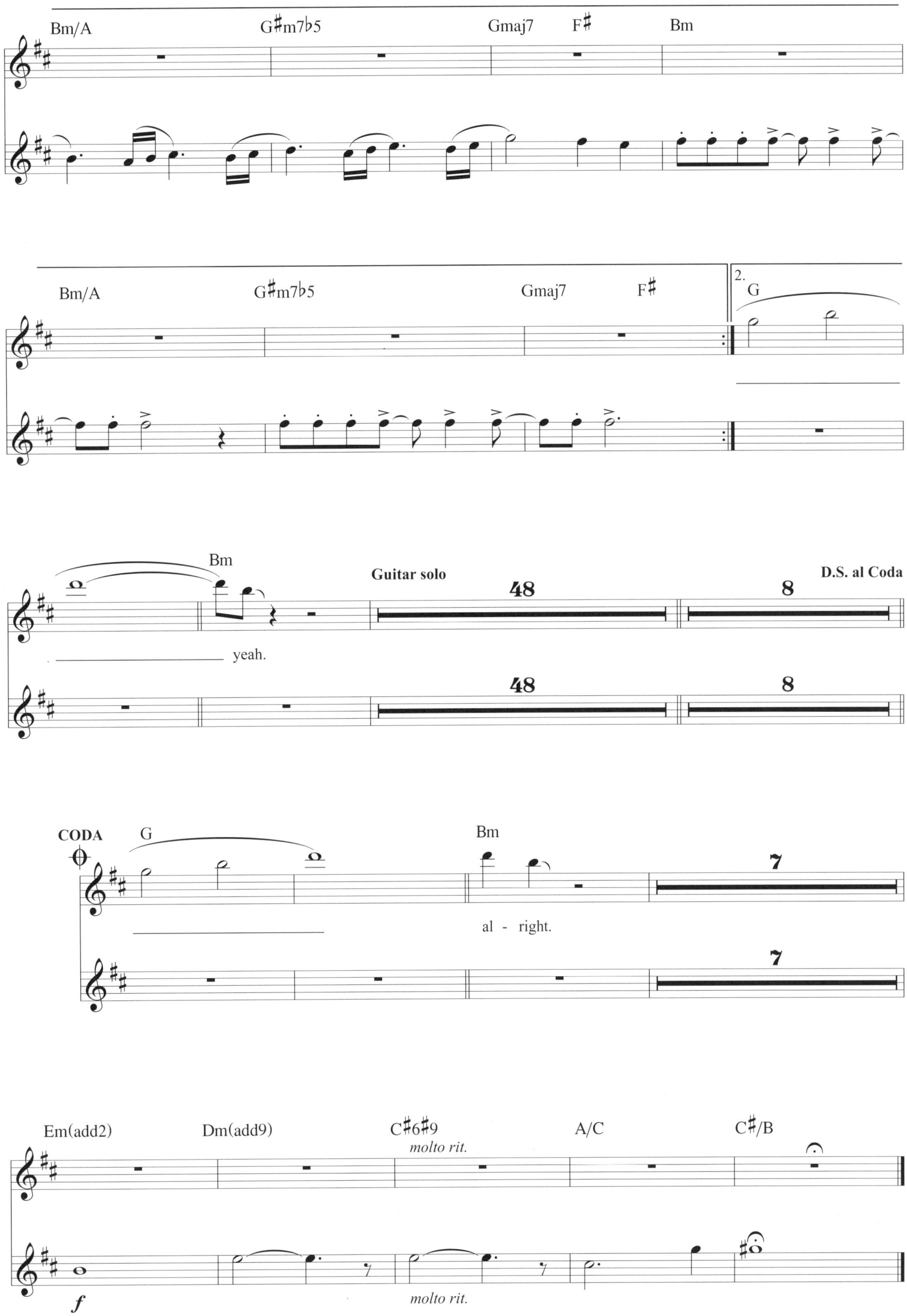
Bm/A
G♯m7♭5
Gmaj7
F♯
Bm
2.
G
Guitar solo
48
8
D.S. al Coda
yeah.
CODA
Bm
7
al - right.
Em(add2)
Dm(add9)
C♯6♯9
molto rit.
A/C
C♯/B
f

# September

Words and Music by Maurice White, Al McKay and Allee Willis

© 1978 EMI APRIL MUSIC INC., STEELCHEST MUSIC, EMI BLACKWOOD MUSIC INC. and IRVING MUSIC INC.
All Rights for STEELCHEST MUSIC Controlled and Administered by EMI APRIL MUSIC INC.
All Rights for IRVING MUSIC INC. Controlled and Administered by EMI BLACKWOOD MUSIC INC.
All Rights Reserved International Copyright Secured Used by Permission

2.
D♯7 D♯7/G G♯m9 B9sus C9sus
stars stole the night a - way?
Hey, hey, hey,
C♯m7 F♯7 D♯m7 G♯m7 C♯m7 F♯7
ba - de - ya, say do you re - mem - ber, ba - de - ya,
f
D♯m7 G♯m7 C♯m7 F♯7 D♯m7 G♯m7
danc - in' in Sep - tem - ber? Ba - de - ya, nev - er was a cloud - y day.
B9sus Emaj7 D♯m7 C♯m7
Ba - doo - doo, ba - doo - doo,
D♯m7 G♯m9 Emaj7 D♯m7 C♯m7 D♯m7 G♯m9
ba - doo - doo, ba - doo - doo, ba - doo - doo, ba - doo, ba - doo - doo, ba - doo - doo,

Emaj7 D♯m7 C♯m7 D♯7/G G♯m9 B9sus
ba - doo-doo, ba - doo, ba - doo - da, doo - day.
f
Emaj7 D♯m7 C♯m7 D♯m7 G♯m9
My thoughts are with you, hold - in' hands with your heart. To see
Emaj7 D♯m7 C♯m7 D♯m7 G♯m9 Emaj7 D♯m7 C♯m7
you, on - ly blue talk and love. Re - mem - ber how we
D♯7 D♯7/G G♯m9 B9sus
knew love was here to stay? Now De -
f
Emaj7 D♯m7 C♯m7 D♯m7 G♯m9 Emaj7 D♯m7 C♯m7
cem - ber, found the love we shared in Sep - tem - ber, on - ly blue
f

D♯m7 G♯m9 Emaj7 D♯m7 C♯m7 D♯7 G♯m9
talk and love. Re - mem - ber, true love we share to - day.
B9sus C9sus C♯m7 F♯7
Hey, hey, hey, ba - de - ya,
Lead vocal ad lib.
f
D♯m7 G♯m7 C♯m7 F♯7 D♯m7 G♯m7
say do you re - mem - ber, ba - de - ya, danc - in' in Sep - tem - ber?
C♯m7 F♯7 D♯m7 G♯m7 B9sus
Ba - de - ya, nev - er was a cloud - y day.
C♯m7 F♯7 D♯m7 G♯m7
And we say ba - de - ya, say do you re - mem - ber,
f

C♯m7 F♯7 D♯m7 G♯m7 C♯m7 F♯7
ba - de - ya, danc - in' in Sep - tem - ber? Ba - de - ya,
D♯m7 G♯m7 B9sus C9sus
gold - en dreams were shin - in' down.
C♯m7 F♯7 D♯m7 G♯m9 C♯m7 F♯7
Now our bells was ring - in', uh - huh. Now our souls were
D♯m7 G♯m9 C♯m7 F♯7 D♯7 G♯m9
sing - in'. Do you re - mem - ber ev - er - y cloud - y day,
B9sus C♯m7 F♯7
yow? And we said ba - de - ya,
ba - de - ya,

D♯m7 G♯m7 C♯m7 F♯7 D♯m7 G♯m7
say do you re-mem-ber, ba-de-ya, danc-in' in Sep-tem-ber?
say do you re-mem-ber, ba-de-ya, danc-in' in Sep-tem-ber?
C♯m7 F♯7 D♯m7 G♯m7 B9sus
Ba-de-ya, nev-er was a cloud-y day.
Ba-de-ya, gold-en dreams were shin-ing down.
1. C9sus 2. C9sus C♯m7 F♯7
And we said Ba-de-ya-de-ya-
f
D♯m7 G♯m9 C♯m7 F♯7 D♯m7 G♯m9
-de-yo, ba-de-ya-de-ya-de-yo,
C♯m7 F♯7 D♯m7 G♯m9 B9sus
Repeat and Fade
ba-de-ya-de-ya-de-yo, de-ya.

# Spinning Wheel

Words and Music by David Clayton Thomas

**Moderate Rock** (♩ = 96)

© 1968 (Renewed 1996) EMI BLACKWOOD MUSIC INC. and BAY MUSIC LTD.
All Rights Controlled and Administered by EMI BLACKWOOD MUSIC INC.
All Rights Reserved International Copyright Secured Used by Permission

F♯7♯9 B13 E7♯9 A13 F♯7♯9 B13
Spin-nin' wheel, all a - lone. Talk - in' 'bout your trou - bles, and ya,
E7♯9 A13 E E7♯9
ya nev-er learn. Ride a paint-ed po - ny, let the spin-nin' wheel turn.
fp
D(add9) C(add9) B♭(add9)
Did you find a di - rect - ing sign on the straight and nar - row
A(add9) D(add9) C(add9)
high - way? Would you mind a re - flect - ing sign? Just
mp
B♭(add9) A B♭/A
let it shine with - in your mind, and show you the
p

Am7/C D E7sus
col - ors that are real.
G7sus Gm11
mf f
F♯7♯9 B13 E7♯9 A13 F♯7♯9 B13
Some - one is wait - in' just for you. Spin-nin' wheel,
f
E7♯9 A13 F♯7♯9 B13 E7♯9 A13
spin - nin' true. Drop all your trou-bles by the riv - er - side.
E E7♯9
Catch a paint-ed po-ny on the spin-nin' wheel ride.
4

Double-time (♩ = 192)
F♯7♯9
B13
E7♯9
A(add2)
8va
Solo Trumpet:
loco
ff
f
F♯7♯9
B13
E7♯9
8va
A(add2)
8va
F♯7♯9
loco
B13
E7♯9
3
A13
F♯7♯9
B13
E7♯9
3
A13
F♯7♯9
8va
(Solo Trumpet cont.)
Trumpet:
f
fp

8va
F7♯9
8va
fp
E7♯9
Freely
Tempo 1
Solo ends
F♯7♯9 B13 E7♯9 A13 F♯7♯9 B13
Some-one's wait-in' just for you. Spin-nin' wheel,
E7♯9 A13 F♯7♯9 B13
spin - nin' true. Drop all your trou - bles by the

E7♯9
A13
E
riv - er - side.
Ride a paint-ed po - ny, let the spin-nin' wheel fly.
F♯7♯9
B
F7♯9
E7♯9
Amaj9
(Lead vocal tacet on repeat)
f
N.C.
F♯7♯9
f
B13
F7♯9
E7♯9
Amaj9
F♯7♯9
B13
F7♯9
E7♯9
Amaj9
Repeat and Fade
f

# Vehicle

Words and Music by James M. Peterik

Copyright © 1969 by BALD MEDUSA MUSIC
Copyright Renewed
International Copyright Secured All Rights Reserved

Fm
I got pic-tures, got can-dy, I'm a lov-a-ble man, and I can
or if you wan-na stay just like you are, you know I
f
Cm7
take you to the near-est star.
think you real-ly should.
Bm
B♭m
I'm your ve-hi-cle, ba - by.
Cm
I'll take you an-y-where you wan-na go.
I'm your
D♭
ve-hi-cle, wom - an.
Csus
By now I'm sure you know
C
B♭m
Cm
D♭
that I love ya, I need ya, I want ya, got to have

Cm
To Coda
1.
Fm
you, child.
Great God in heav - en, you know I love
you.
Cm7
Fm
Cm7
Well, if you
2.
Fm
Great God in heav - en, you know I love
you.
Cm7
Aw, you know I do.
Fm

Cm7
8
B♭m
Cm
D♭
Csus
C
B♭m
Cm
D♭
C
Fm
Cm7
Fm
Cm7
D.S. al Coda
Well, I'm the
CODA
Fm
Great God in heav - en, you know I love
you.
Cm7
And I'm your

Fm
ve - hi - cle, babe. Al - right.
Cm7
Ya know I love ya, I need, ya,
B♭m
Cm
I want you, got to have you, child.
D♭
Cm
Slowly
Fm
Great God in heav - en, you know I love you.
A tempo
Fm
Cm7
Fm

HAL•LEONARD®

# TRUMPET PLAY-ALONG

*The Trumpet Play-Along Series will help you play your favorite songs quickly and easily. Just follow the printed music, listen to the sound-alike recordings and hear how the trumpet should sound, and then play along using the separate backing tracks.*

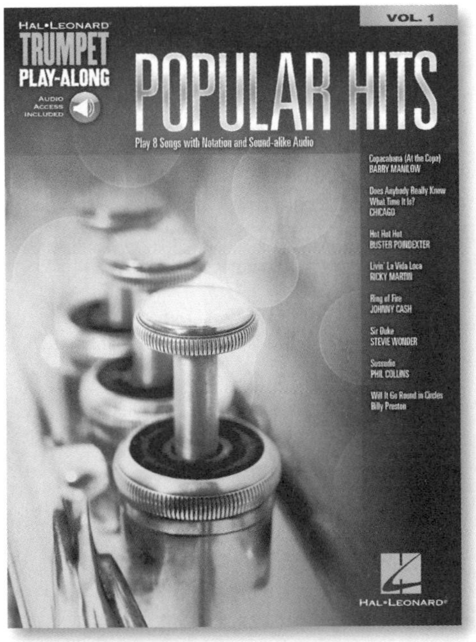


**1. POPULAR HITS**

Copacabana (At the Copa) (Barry Manilow) • Does Anybody Really Know What Time It Is? (Chicago) • Hot Hot Hot (Buster Poindexter) • Livin' La Vida Loca (Ricky Martin) • Ring of Fire (Johnny Cash) • Sir Duke (Stevie Wonder) • Sussudio (Phil Collins) • Will It Go Round in Circles (Billy Preston).

00137383
Book/Online Audio
$16.99

**2. TRUMPET CLASSICS**

Ciribiribin (Harry James) • Feels So Good (Chuck Mangione) • Java (Al Hirt) • Music to Watch Girls By (Bob Crewe Generation) • Spanish Flea (Herb Alpert) • Sugar Blues (Al Hirt) • A Taste of Honey (Herb Alpert) • The Toy Trumpet (Raymond Scott).

00137384
Book/Online Audio
$16.99

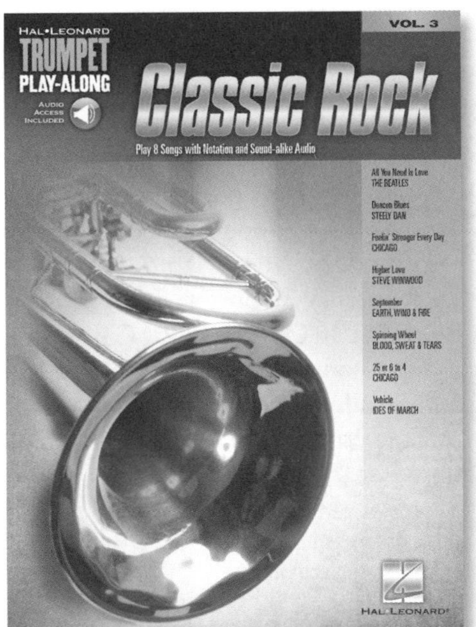


**3. CLASSIC ROCK**

All You Need Is Love (The Beatles) • Deacon Blues (Steely Dan) • Feelin' Stronger Every Day (Chicago) • Higher Love (Steve Winwood) • September (Earth, Wind & Fire) • Spinning Wheel (Blood, Sweat & Tears) • 25 or 6 to 4 (Chicago) • Vehicle (Ides of March).

00137385
Book/Online Audio
$16.99

**4. GREAT THEMES**

Cherry Pink and Apple Blossom White (Perez Prado) • Deborah's Theme (Ennio Morricone) • Dragnet (Walter Schumann) • The Godfather Waltz (Nino Rota) • Gonna Fly Now (Bill Conti) • Green Hornet Theme (Al Hirt) • The Odd Couple (Neal Hefti) • Sugar Lips (Al Hirt).

00137386
Book/Online Audio
$16.99

HAL•LEONARD®
CORPORATION
7777 W. BLUEMOUND RD. P.O. BOX 13819 MILWAUKEE, WI 53213

Prices, contents, and availability subject to change without notice.

www.halleonard.com

1114

NOTE-FOR-NOTE TRANSCRIPTIONS • FROM THE ORIGINAL RECORDINGS •

# transcribed horns

Imagine playing the exact parts of some of the most memorable and consequential songs of our time note-for-note, exactly as the legends played them. This unique series features transcriptions of all the horn parts included on the original recordings.

## FUNK/DISCO HORN SECTION

15 classics: Brick House • Disco Inferno • Dr. Funkenstein • Fire • Give It to Me Baby • Hold On I'm Comin' • Lucretia Mac Evil • Papa's Got a Brand New Bag • Pick up the Pieces • Serpentine Fire • Superstition • That's the Way (I Like It) • Y.M.C.A. • You Should Be Dancing • What Is Hip.

00001148 ....................$19.95

## POP/ROCK HORN SECTION

15 great hits: Bright Side of the Road • Higher Love • Hot Hot Hot • The Impression That I Get • Jump, Jive An' Wail • Livin' La Vida Loca • Magical Mystery Tour • Peg • Smooth • Spinning Wheel • Sussudio • 25 or 6 to 4 • Vehicle • Will It Go Round in Circles • Zoot Suit Riot.

00001149 ....................$19.95

## R&B HORN SECTION

15 R&B standards: Cut the Cake • Dancing in the Street • Gimme Some Lovin' • Hallelujah I Love Him So • Hard to Handle • I Got You (I Feel Good) • In the Midnight Hour • It's Your Thing • Knock on Wood • Mustang Sally • September • Sir Duke • Soul Finger • Soul Man • You've Made Me So Very Happy.

00001147 ....................$19.95

## JAZZ/POP HORN SECTION

15 jazzy favorites: After the Love Has Gone • Birdland • Deacon Blues • Doin' It (All for My Baby) • Fantasy • Got to Get You into My Life • Grazing in the Grass • In the Navy • The Madison Time • My Old School • Spanish Flea • Tell Her About It • Tijuana Taxi • What You Won't Do for Love • You Can't Get What You Want (Till You Know What You Want).

00001503 ....................$19.99

## JAZZ/ROCK HORN SECTION

14 rockin' gems: And When I Die • Does Anybody Really Know What Time It Is? • Feelin' Stronger Every Day • Get It On • Honky Cat • The Horse • The Letter • Make Me Smile • Mercy, Mercy, Mercy • Proud Mary • Shake a Tail Feather • So Very Hard to Go • Watermelon Man • Yellow Submarine.

00001504 ....................$19.99


HAL•LEONARD®
CORPORATION

7777 W. BLUEMOUND RD. P.O. BOX 13819 MILWAUKEE, WI 53213

www.halleonard.com



Prices, contents and availability subject to change without notice.

0112

## HAL•LEONARD INSTRUMENTAL PLAY-ALONG

Your favorite songs are arranged just for solo instrumentalists with this outstanding series. Each book includes a great full-accompaniment play-along CD so you can sound just like a pro! Check out **www.halleonard.com** to see all the titles available.

### Disney Greats

Arabian Nights • Hawaiian Roller Coaster Ride • It's a Small World • Look Through My Eyes • Yo Ho (A Pirate's Life for Me) • and more.

______00841934 Flute . . . . . . . . . . . . . . . . $12.95
______00841935 Clarinet . . . . . . . . . . . . . . $12.95
______00841936 Alto Sax . . . . . . . . . . . . . . $12.95
______00841937 Tenor Sax . . . . . . . . . . . . $12.95
______00841938 Trumpet. . . . . . . . . . . . . . $12.95
______00841939 Horn . . . . . . . . . . . . . . . . $12.95
______00841940 Trombone . . . . . . . . . . . . $12.95
______00841941 Violin. . . . . . . . . . . . . . . . $12.95
______00841942 Viola . . . . . . . . . . . . . . . . $12.95
______00841943 Cello . . . . . . . . . . . . . . . . $12.95
______00842078 Oboe . . . . . . . . . . . . . . . . $12.95

### Glee

And I Am Telling You I'm Not Going • Defying Gravity • Don't Stop Believin' • Keep Holding On • Lean on Me • No Air • Sweet Caroline • True Colors • and more.

______00842479 Flute . . . . . . . . . . . . . . . . $12.99
______00842480 Clarinet . . . . . . . . . . . . . . $12.99
______00842481 Alto Sax . . . . . . . . . . . . . . $12.99
______00842482 Tenor Sax . . . . . . . . . . . . $12.99
______00842483 Trumpet. . . . . . . . . . . . . . $12.99
______00842484 Horn . . . . . . . . . . . . . . . . $12.99
______00842485 Trombone . . . . . . . . . . . . $12.99
______00842486 Violin. . . . . . . . . . . . . . . . $12.99
______00842487 Viola . . . . . . . . . . . . . . . . $12.99
______00842488 Cello . . . . . . . . . . . . . . . . $12.99

### Motown Classics

ABC • Endless Love • I Just Called to Say I Love You • My Girl • The Tracks of My Tears • What's Going On • You've Really Got a Hold on Me • and more.

______00842572 Flute . . . . . . . . . . . . . . . . $12.99
______00842573 Clarinet . . . . . . . . . . . . . . $12.99
______00842574 Alto Saxophone . . . . . . . . $12.99
______00842575 Tenor Saxophone. . . . . . . $12.99
______00842576 Trumpet. . . . . . . . . . . . . . $12.99
______00842577 Horn . . . . . . . . . . . . . . . . $12.99
______00842578 Trombone . . . . . . . . . . . . $12.99
______00842579 Violin. . . . . . . . . . . . . . . . $12.99
______00842580 Viola . . . . . . . . . . . . . . . . $12.99
______00842581 Cello . . . . . . . . . . . . . . . . $12.99

### Popular Hits

Breakeven • Fireflies • Halo • Hey, Soul Sister • I Gotta Feeling • I'm Yours • Need You Now • Poker Face • Viva La Vida • You Belong with Me • and more.

______00842511 Flute . . . . . . . . . . . . . . . . $12.99
______00842512 Clarinet . . . . . . . . . . . . . . $12.99
______00842513 Alto Sax . . . . . . . . . . . . . . $12.99
______00842514 Tenor Sax . . . . . . . . . . . . $12.99
______00842515 Trumpet. . . . . . . . . . . . . . $12.99
______00842516 Horn . . . . . . . . . . . . . . . . $12.99
______00842517 Trombone . . . . . . . . . . . . $12.99
______00842518 Violin. . . . . . . . . . . . . . . . $12.99
______00842519 Viola . . . . . . . . . . . . . . . . $12.99
______00842520 Cello . . . . . . . . . . . . . . . . $12.99

### Sports Rock

Another One Bites the Dust • Centerfold • Crazy Train • Get Down Tonight • Let's Get It Started • Shout • The Way You Move • and more.

______00842326 Flute . . . . . . . . . . . . . . . . $12.99
______00842327 Clarinet . . . . . . . . . . . . . . $12.99
______00842328 Alto Sax . . . . . . . . . . . . . . $12.99
______00842329 Tenor Sax . . . . . . . . . . . . $12.99
______00842330 Trumpet. . . . . . . . . . . . . . $12.99
______00842331 Horn . . . . . . . . . . . . . . . . $12.99
______00842332 Trombone . . . . . . . . . . . . $12.99
______00842333 Violin. . . . . . . . . . . . . . . . $12.99
______00842334 Viola . . . . . . . . . . . . . . . . $12.99
______00842335 Cello . . . . . . . . . . . . . . . . $12.99

### Women of Pop

Bad Romance • Jar of Hearts • Mean • My Life Would Suck Without You • Our Song • Rolling in the Deep • Single Ladies (Put a Ring on It) • Teenage Dream • and more.

______00842650 Flute . . . . . . . . . . . . . . . . $12.99
______00842651 Clarinet . . . . . . . . . . . . . . $12.99
______00842652 Alto Sax . . . . . . . . . . . . . . $12.99
______00842653 Tenor Sax . . . . . . . . . . . . $12.99
______00842654 Trumpet. . . . . . . . . . . . . . $12.99
______00842655 Horn . . . . . . . . . . . . . . . . $12.99
______00842656 Trombone . . . . . . . . . . . . $12.99
______00842657 Violin. . . . . . . . . . . . . . . . $12.99
______00842658 Viola . . . . . . . . . . . . . . . . $12.99
______00842659 Cello . . . . . . . . . . . . . . . . $12.99

### Twilight

Bella's Lullaby • Decode • Eyes on Fire • Full Moon • Go All the Way (Into the Twilight) • Leave Out All the Rest • Spotlight (Twilight Remix) • Supermassive Black Hole • Tremble for My Beloved.

______00842406 Flute . . . . . . . . . . . . . . . . $12.99
______00842407 Clarinet . . . . . . . . . . . . . . $12.99
______00842408 Alto Sax . . . . . . . . . . . . . . $12.99
______00842409 Tenor Sax . . . . . . . . . . . . $12.99
______00842410 Trumpet. . . . . . . . . . . . . . $12.99
______00842411 Horn . . . . . . . . . . . . . . . . $12.99
______00842412 Trombone . . . . . . . . . . . . $12.99
______00842413 Violin. . . . . . . . . . . . . . . . $12.99
______00842414 Viola . . . . . . . . . . . . . . . . $12.99
______00842415 Cello . . . . . . . . . . . . . . . . $12.99

### Twilight – New Moon

Almost a Kiss • Dreamcatcher • Edward Leaves • I Need You • Memories of Edward • New Moon • Possibility • Roslyn • Satellite Heart • and more.

______00842458 Flute . . . . . . . . . . . . . . . . $12.99
______00842459 Clarinet . . . . . . . . . . . . . . $12.99
______00842460 Alto Sax . . . . . . . . . . . . . . $12.99
______00842461 Tenor Sax . . . . . . . . . . . . $12.99
______00842462 Trumpet. . . . . . . . . . . . . . $12.99
______00842463 Horn . . . . . . . . . . . . . . . . $12.99
______00842464 Trombone . . . . . . . . . . . . $12.99
______00842465 Violin. . . . . . . . . . . . . . . . $12.99
______00842466 Viola . . . . . . . . . . . . . . . . $12.99
______00842467 Cello . . . . . . . . . . . . . . . . $12.99

### Wicked

As Long As You're Mine • Dancing Through Life • Defying Gravity • For Good • I'm Not That Girl • Popular • The Wizard and I • and more.

______00842236 Book/CD Pack. . . . . . . . . $11.95
______00842237 Book/CD Pack. . . . . . . . . $11.95
______00842238 Alto Saxophone . . . . . . . . $11.95
______00842239 Tenor Saxophone. . . . . . . $11.95
______00842240 Trumpet. . . . . . . . . . . . . . $11.95
______00842241 Horn . . . . . . . . . . . . . . . . $11.95
______00842242 Trombone . . . . . . . . . . . . $11.95
______00842243 Violin. . . . . . . . . . . . . . . . $11.95
______00842244 Viola . . . . . . . . . . . . . . . . $11.95
______00842245 Cello . . . . . . . . . . . . . . . . $11.95


For More Information, See Your Local Music Dealer, Or Write To:

HAL•LEONARD® CORPORATION

7777 W. Bluemound Rd. P.O. Box 13819 Milwaukee, WI 53213

Prices, contents, and availability subject to change without notice.
Disney characters and artwork © Disney Enterprises, Inc.

# The Best-Selling Jazz Book of All Time Is Now Legal!

The Real Books are the most popular jazz books of all time. Since the 1970s, musicians have trusted these volumes to get them through every gig, night after night. The problem is that the books were illegally produced and distributed, without any regard to copyright law, or royalties paid to the composers who created these musical masterpieces.

Hal Leonard is very proud to present the first legitimate and legal editions of these books ever produced. You won't even notice the difference, other than all the notorious errors being fixed: the covers and typeface look the same, the song lists are nearly identical, and the price for our edition is even cheaper than the originals!

Every conscientious musician will appreciate that these books are now produced accurately and ethically, benefitting the songwriters that we owe for some of the greatest tunes of all time!

**VOLUME 1**

| | | |
|---|---|---|
| 00240221 | C Edition | $35.00 |
| 00240224 | B♭ Edition | $35.00 |
| 00240225 | E♭ Edition | $35.00 |
| 00240226 | Bass Clef Edition | $35.00 |
| 00240292 | C Edition 6 x 9 | $30.00 |
| 00240339 | B♭ Edition 6 x 9 | $30.00 |
| 00451087 | C Edition on CD-ROM | $25.00 |
| 00240302 | A-D CD Backing Tracks | $24.99 |
| 00240303 | E-J CD Backing Tracks | $24.95 |
| 00240304 | L-R CD Backing Tracks | $24.95 |
| 00240305 | S-Z CD Backing Tracks | $24.99 |
| 00110604 | Book/USB Flash Drive Backing Tracks Pack | $79.99 |
| 00110599 | USB Flash Drive Only | $50.00 |

**VOLUME 2**

| | | |
|---|---|---|
| 00240222 | C Edition | $35.50 |
| 00240227 | B♭ Edition | $35.00 |
| 00240228 | E♭ Edition | $35.00 |
| 00240229 | Bass Clef Edition | $35.00 |
| 00240293 | C Edition 6 x 9 | $30.00 |
| 00125900 | B♭ Edition 6 x 9 | $30.00 |
| 00451088 | C Edition on CD-ROM | $27.99 |
| 00240351 | A-D CD Backing Tracks | $24.99 |
| 00240352 | E-I CD Backing Tracks | $24.99 |
| 00240353 | J-R CD Backing Tracks | $24.99 |
| 00240354 | S-Z CD Backing Tracks | $24.99 |

**VOLUME 3**

| | | |
|---|---|---|
| 00240233 | C Edition | $35.00 |
| 00240284 | B♭ Edition | $35.00 |
| 00240285 | E♭ Edition | $35.00 |
| 00240286 | Bass Clef Edition | $35.00 |
| 00240338 | C Edition 6 x 9 | $30.00 |
| 00451089 | C Edition on CD-ROM | $29.99 |

**VOLUME 4**

| | | |
|---|---|---|
| 00240296 | C Edition | $35.00 |
| 00103348 | B♭ Edition | $35.00 |
| 00103349 | E♭ Edition | $35.00 |
| 00103350 | Bass Clef Edition | $35.00 |

**VOLUME 5**

| | | |
|---|---|---|
| 00240349 | C Edition | $35.00 |

***Also available:***

| | | |
|---|---|---|
| 00240264 | The Real Blues Book | $34.99 |
| 00310910 | The Real Bluegrass Book | $29.99 |
| 00240440 | The Trane Book | $22.99 |
| 00240137 | Miles Davis Real Book | $19.95 |
| 00240355 | The Real Dixieland Book | $29.99 |
| 00122335 | The Real Dixieland Book B♭ Edition | $29.99 |
| 00240235 | The Duke Ellington Real Book | $19.99 |
| 00240268 | The Real Jazz Solos Book | $30.00 |
| 00240348 | The Real Latin Book | $35.00 |
| 00127107 | The Real Latin Book B♭ Edition | $35.00 |
| 00240358 | The Charlie Parker Real Book | $19.99 |
| 00240331 | The Bud Powell Real Book | $19.99 |
| 00240313 | The Real Rock Book | $35.00 |
| 00240323 | The Real Rock Book – Vol. 2 | $35.00 |
| 00240359 | The Real Tab Book | $32.50 |
| 00240317 | The Real Worship Book | $29.99 |

**THE REAL CHRISTMAS BOOK**

| | | |
|---|---|---|
| 00240306 | C Edition | $29.99 |
| 00240345 | B♭ Edition | $29.99 |
| 00240346 | E♭ Edition | $29.99 |
| 00240347 | Bass Clef Edition | $29.99 |
| 00240431 | A-G CD Backing Tracks | $24.99 |
| 00240432 | H-M CD Backing Tracks | $24.99 |
| 00240433 | N-Y CD Backing Tracks | $24.99 |

**THE REAL VOCAL BOOK**

| | | |
|---|---|---|
| 00240230 | Volume 1 High Voice | $35.00 |
| 00240307 | Volume 1 Low Voice | $35.00 |
| 00240231 | Volume 2 High Voice | $35.00 |
| 00240308 | Volume 2 Low Voice | $35.00 |
| 00240391 | Volume 3 High Voice | $35.00 |
| 00240392 | Volume 3 Low Voice | $35.00 |

**THE REAL BOOK – STAFF PAPER**

00240327 ........ $10.99

**HOW TO PLAY FROM A REAL BOOK**

For All Musicians

*by Robert Rawlins*

00312097 ........ $17.50

**Complete song lists online at www.halleonard.com**

*Prices, content, and availability subject to change without notice.*

HAL•LEONARD® CORPORATION

7777 W. Bluemound Rd. P.O. Box 13819 Milwaukee, WI 53213

0714